THE UNSEEN REALM IS REAL

A Complete Guide to Spiritual Warfare & Discernment

Volume A: Foundations

Volume B: Advanced Assignments

By Tavaca Dorsey

THE UNSEEN REALM IS REAL

A Complete Guide to Spiritual Warfare & Discernment

Scripture quotations are taken from the King James Version of the Bible, which is in the public domain.

ISBN: 979-8-9939537-1-7

DEDICATED TO

The ones who always felt 'something was there'—but had no language, no teacher, no validation, and no vocabulary for what they were sensing.

You were not imagining it.

You were not overreacting.

You were not weak.

You were not dramatic.

You were discerning.

This book is for your awakening.

TABLE OF CONTENTS

DEDICATED TO

The ones who always felt 'something was there'—but had no language, no teacher, no validation, and no vocabulary for what they were sensing.

You were not imagining it.

You were not overreacting.

You were not weak.

You were not dramatic.

You were discerning.

This book is for your awakening.

INTRODUCTION

A Beginner's Manual for Seeing the Invisible World

This volume speaks to believers, unbelievers, wounded people, confused people, spiritually curious people, and people who've lived through things without language.

If you've ever walked into a room and felt something you couldn't explain...

If you've ever been in the presence of someone who shifted the entire atmosphere just by being there...

If you've ever experienced unexplained exhaustion, sudden fear, or an invisible weight pressing on your spirit...

Then you've already encountered the unseen realm.

You just didn't have the language to name it.

Most people spend their entire lives reacting to invisible forces they never learned to identify. They blame themselves for mood swings that weren't theirs. They accept fatigue that has no natural explanation. They tolerate relationships that drain their very soul, never realizing they're under spiritual attack.

This book exists to give you eyes to see what's really happening.

You cannot fight what you cannot name. You cannot resist what you cannot see. And you cannot overcome what you do not understand.

The unseen realm is not fantasy, superstition, or imagination. It is the real world behind the one we touch. Everything that happens in the natural finds its roots in the spiritual first.

Think about it: Before an argument erupts in the physical, tension builds in the spiritual. Before depression manifests in your emotions, oppression settled in the atmosphere around you. Before betrayal happens in a relationship, a spirit of division was already at work.

The physical realm is simply the manifestation of what's already been decided, influenced, or battled in the unseen.

This is your awakening:

Your life has never been random. Nothing 'just happened.' You were interacting with an invisible world without knowing it. Every unexplained mood shift, every sudden drain of energy, every person who made you uncomfortable for reasons you couldn't articulate—these weren't accidents. They were encounters with the unseen realm.

And God is now giving you eyes to finally see.

This is not a theoretical book. This is a practical guide born from lived experience, spiritual warfare, and hard-won understanding. In these pages, you will learn:

- How to recognize when you've entered a spiritually charged atmosphere—and what to do about it
- The difference between your own emotions and spiritual interference operating through external forces
- How the enemy works through people, placements, and patterns—not the horror-movie demons most expect
- The most common spiritual tactics you face daily: jealousy, mimicry, siphoning, fatigue, confusion, and isolation
- How to develop the gift of discernment and learn to trust your spiritual radar
- How prayer shifts atmospheres and why timing matters more than you realize in spiritual warfare
- Your spiritual identity and authority—and how to reclaim your soul, strength, and voice from forces that have been draining them

But more than just knowledge, you will gain something even more valuable: You will gain the ability to recognize what's been happening to you all along.

That unexplained exhaustion after being around certain people? That wasn't you being weak. That was energy siphoning.

That sudden confusion that clouded your thinking right before a major decision? That wasn't you being indecisive. That was a spirit of confusion assigned to derail you.

That person who seemed friendly but always left you feeling drained and unsettled? That wasn't your imagination. That was discernment alerting you to a spiritual assignment.

This book will give you language for what you've been experiencing. And language is power. Because once you can name what's happening, you can resist it. Once you can see it, you can fight it. Once you understand it, you can overcome it.

Why This Book Exists

I didn't write this book because I wanted to. I wrote it because I had to.

For years, I lived through spiritual warfare that I couldn't explain. I encountered invisible forces, felt atmospheric shifts, discerned assignments on people, and experienced spiritual attacks—all while having no framework to understand what was happening to me.

The church didn't talk about it. My friends couldn't relate to it. The world dismissed it as paranoia or mental instability. I was left to navigate the unseen realm alone, learning through trial and error, through mistakes and breakthroughs, through attacks and victories.

And then God began to give me language.

Not academic language. Not religious jargon. But clear, practical, accessible language that everyday people could understand and apply.

I realized that millions of people are living through the same thing I experienced—sensing the unseen, feeling spiritual dynamics, encountering invisible warfare—but they have no vocabulary for it. They think they're crazy. They think they're alone. They think something is wrong with them.

Nothing is wrong with you. You're not crazy. You're not paranoid. You're not overly sensitive.

You're spiritually aware. And that awareness has been trying to protect you, warn you, and guide you—but you didn't have the framework to trust it.

This book is that framework.

This Is Not a Book About Fear

Let me be clear from the beginning: This is not a fear-based manual. This is an awareness-based equipping.

The purpose of this book is not to magnify darkness, but to expose it—clearly, simply, and intelligently—so that believers and seekers alike may recognize, resist, and rise above spiritual interference with confidence.

Fear comes from not knowing. Fear comes from being blindsided. Fear comes from feeling powerless against forces you can't see or understand.

But once you understand how the unseen realm operates, fear dissolves. It's replaced with clarity. With authority. With strategic wisdom.

You're not learning this information so you can be afraid of every room you walk into. You're learning it so you can walk into every room with eyes wide open, spirit alert, and discernment activated.

You're not learning this so you can become paranoid about people. You're learning it so you can recognize assignments, set boundaries, and protect your peace without guilt.

You're not learning this to live in constant battle mode. You're learning it so you can live in constant awareness—which actually brings more peace, not less.

Because the most dangerous place to be is not in spiritual warfare. The most dangerous place to be is in spiritual warfare while being completely blind to it.

This book removes the blindfold.

This is a guidebook, not just a book to read once and put on a shelf.

Keep it close. Keep it accessible. Return to it when:

- You walk into an atmosphere that feels off and need to understand what you're sensing
- You encounter a person who drains you and need to know how to respond
- You're experiencing unexplained fatigue, confusion, or oppression
- You need to cleanse your spiritual space and don't know where to start
- You're in a season of spiritual attack and need practical strategies

This book is designed to be referenced, not just read. Mark it up. Highlight sections that resonate. Dog-ear pages you need to return to. Write notes in the margins. Make this book yours.

And as you read, pay attention to what your spirit highlights. Not every chapter will land the same for every reader. Some sections will feel like they were written specifically for you. That's God speaking. That's revelation meeting experience. That's your awakening beginning.

You're about to learn how to see what's been invisible. You're about to gain language for what you've been experiencing. You're about to understand spiritual dynamics that most people live and die without ever recognizing.

This is not just information. This is transformation.

This is your awakening to the unseen realm.

It's time to see clearly. It's time to understand what you've been sensing all along. It's time to walk in authority, move in wisdom, and live free from invisible forces you never learned to resist.

Welcome to the foundations of spiritual warfare.

Let's begin.

SECTION I
AWAKENING TO THE INVISIBLE REALM

Before you can engage in spiritual warfare, you must first awaken to the reality that there is a war happening.

Most people live their entire lives asleep to the unseen realm— reacting to spiritual attacks without ever understanding what hit them, absorbing atmospheres without recognizing contamination, and accepting spiritual interference as 'just life.'

This section removes the veil.

CHAPTER 1

The Unseen Realm Is Real

Most people live their entire lives reacting to what they can see, never realizing that the true battle was never in the natural.

Arguments, atmospheres, tension, sudden depression, unexplained fear, fatigue that makes no sense—the world calls them 'mood swings,' 'intuition,' or 'life happening.'

But in reality, something far deeper is moving.

You felt it long before you had the language for it.

A pressure in the air.

A shift in someone's eyes.

An unspoken heaviness in a room.

A knowing in your spirit that something wasn't right—even if everyone else shrugged it off.

What You've Been Experiencing

These moments of sensing aren't imagination. They aren't paranoia. They aren't you being 'too sensitive' or 'overthinking things.'

They are your spirit responding to the unseen realm—a dimension of reality that operates parallel to the physical world but with far greater influence over what actually happens in your life.

Every physical event has a spiritual root. Every atmosphere carries spiritual information. Every encounter involves invisible forces you cannot see with natural eyes.

The unseen realm is not some mystical concept reserved for prophets and seers. It's the operating system of reality itself. And whether you acknowledge it or not, you interact with it every single day.

Consider this: When you walk into a room and immediately feel uncomfortable, what's really happening? Your spirit is reading the atmosphere before your mind can process it. When you meet someone who seems nice but something in you resists them, what's that about? Your discernment is picking up on spiritual dynamics your eyes can't see.

When you suddenly feel drained after being around certain people, that's not coincidence. When specific locations make you feel heavy or oppressed, that's not your imagination. When you can't shake a feeling that something is wrong even though everything looks fine, that's not paranoia.

That's the unseen realm making itself known to you.

The enemy's greatest weapon is not attack—it's blindness.

If he can keep you from seeing what's really happening, he doesn't have to fight you at all. You'll fight yourself. You'll blame yourself. You'll exhaust yourself trying to fix problems in the natural realm that are rooted in the spiritual.

Most people are taught to:

- Ignore their spiritual instincts
- Rationalize away discernment
- Dismiss spiritual warfare as superstition
- Accept exhaustion, confusion, and oppression as 'just life'

This conditioning begins early. Children naturally sense the unseen realm—they feel when something is 'off,' when a person carries darkness, when an atmosphere is heavy. But instead of being trained to trust their discernment, they're told:

'There's nothing there.'

'You're being dramatic.'

'Stop being afraid of nothing.'

'It's all in your head.'

Over time, that spiritual sensitivity gets muted. The soul develops what can only be described as curtains—layers of conditioning that block the natural ability to perceive spiritual reality.

By adulthood, most people have completely lost access to their spiritual radar. They sense things but override them. They feel warnings but rationalize them away. They know something is wrong but have no framework to understand it.

And so they live blind. Walking through a spiritually active world while seeing none of it. Engaging with people carrying assignments while recognizing none of them. Absorbing oppressive atmospheres while questioning none of it.

They assume that what they experience physically is all there is. They never consider that behind every conversation, there's a spiritual dynamic. Behind every relationship, there's an invisible influence. Behind every atmosphere, there's a spiritual climate that was created by something—or someone.

This book exists to remove those curtains and restore your ability to see.

The Three Levels of Spiritual Awareness

Understanding the unseen realm begins with recognizing three distinct levels of spiritual awareness.

Level 1: Unconscious Interaction

This is where most people operate. They're constantly affected by spiritual forces but have no conscious awareness of it. They walk through spiritually contaminated spaces and absorb oppression without realizing it.

At this level, the unseen realm has full access to influence your life while you remain completely blind to what's happening.

Level 2: Sensing Without Understanding

This is where spiritual awakening begins. You start noticing patterns. You feel when something is off even if you can't explain it.

This is actually a dangerous stage because discernment without wisdom can lead to fear, paranoia, or constant spiritual anxiety.

Level 3: Discernment With Understanding

This is spiritual maturity. You not only sense what's happening—you understand it. You recognize tactics, identify spirits, and respond strategically instead of reacting emotionally.

This book is designed to move you from Level 1 to Level 3 progressively and deliberately.

What This Journey Will Cost You

Before we go further, understand this: once you begin to see the unseen realm, you cannot unsee it.

This awareness will change how you view people, how you move through the world, and your expectations of others. Some relationships will reveal themselves as spiritually toxic. You'll recognize assignments disguised as friendships.

And people won't understand. They'll think you're being antisocial or paranoid.

But you will gain something far more valuable: freedom from manipulation, spiritual exhaustion, and invisible forces controlling your life.

The unseen realm is real. And now that you know it exists, your life will never be the same.

CHAPTER 2

How the Invisible Interferes With the Everyday

The unseen realm does not wait for dramatic moments. It works quietly, consistently, subtly—woven into everyday life.

The spirit world expresses itself through personalities, atmospheres, timing, patterns, and access points. Not theatrics.

1. Atmospheres Carry Messages

You've walked into rooms that felt 'off.' That was discernment alerting you that the atmosphere had been tampered with.

Atmospheres can be:

- Heavy — oppression or unresolved darkness
- Tense — conflict or spiritual opposition
- Agitated — spiritual manipulation
- Draining — energy siphoning or monitoring spirits
- Peaceful — divine presence or protection

Your spirit senses what your eyes can't see. Two identical rooms can feel completely different because of their spiritual climate.

2. People Can Carry Assignments

Not everyone who enters your life is sent by God.

Assignments can appear as:

- Coworkers who drain your energy
- Supervisors who inexplicably oppose you
- Friends who subtly compete or mimic you
- People who appear at critical moments repeatedly

Discernment is about recognizing what people are carrying, not judging their hearts.

3. Timing Is Never Random

Pay attention to when things happen. Attacks don't randomly coincide with breakthroughs. Opposition doesn't accidentally intensify before promotions.

Notice when:

- Conflict erupts right before significant events
- Exhaustion hits before important steps
- Confusion clouds critical decisions
- Fear grips you before forward movement

These patterns are not bad luck—they're spiritual interference designed to derail you before you reach your destination.

One incident is an event. Multiple incidents with the same theme is a pattern. Patterns reveal spiritual assignments.

If you keep experiencing betrayal, sabotage, isolation, or unexplained setbacks—these aren't personality flaws or bad luck. These are manifestations of spiritual warfare through patterns designed to keep you stuck.

The unseen realm operates through access points—spiritual doors that grant permission for influence:

- Sin — ongoing disobedience creates legal ground
- Trauma — unhealed wounds become entry points
- Agreements — believing lies about yourself or God
- Unforgiveness — binds you to those who hurt you
- Soul ties — ungodly connections allowing spiritual transfer

When you close the doors the enemy's been using, his influence diminishes significantly.

The invisible realm doesn't interfere randomly. It operates through deliberate, strategic methods.

CHAPTER 3

Every physical environment has an unseen spiritual climate attached to it.

Atmospheres are not created by walls or décor. They're created by presence, agreement, activities, and history.

When you enter a place, you're entering a spiritual narrative already in progress.

Atmospheres are not neutral. Every space is spiritually occupied—either by light or darkness, peace or oppression.

What Creates an Atmosphere

1. Words Spoken

Words are spiritual containers releasing life or death. A home with constant arguing carries verbal violence residue. Conversely, homes saturated with prayer carry peace.

2. Actions Conducted

What happens in a space leaves spiritual imprints. Violence creates trauma. Sexual sin opens doors to perversion. Worship invites divine presence.

3. Spirits Welcomed

Occult practices, idolatry, sexual immorality, and violence create legal ground for demonic occupation. Spirits don't leave until actively driven out.

4. Covenants Made

Marriage covenants, business partnerships, even casual agreements ('I'll never forgive them') create spiritual contracts that shape atmospheres.

5. Authority Assigned

Whoever has spiritual authority over a space determines its atmosphere. Authority creates atmospheres. Whoever controls the atmosphere controls the outcome.

6. People Who Dwell There

People filled with the Holy Spirit bring light. People bound by depression create heaviness. One toxic person can shift an entire household.

Atmospheres don't lie—people do.

How to Read Atmospheres

When you enter a space, notice:

- How your body responds (tension, peace, heaviness)
- How your mood shifts (sudden sadness, irritation, joy)
- How your energy changes (drained or renewed)
- Whether you want to stay or leave immediately

These responses are spiritual intelligence, not random feelings.

Cleansing Contaminated Atmospheres

If you discern a space is contaminated:

- Pray and declare God's authority over the space
- Use anointing oil if available
- Play worship music
- Open windows (symbolically releasing what's trapped)
- Speak life and scripture

Your authority as a believer can shift any atmosphere God assigns you to occupy.

If you only assess rooms with your eyes, you'll miss what your spirit is warning you about.

In the next chapter, we'll explore how the soul can be blindfolded—how spiritual sensitivity gets muted and what restores it.

SESSION 2

Chapters 4-6

Continuing Section I & Beginning Section II

CHAPTER 4

How the Soul Can Be Blindfolded

There is a phenomenon that occurs in the spiritual realm that most people never recognize: the soul can be blindfolded.

This isn't about physical sight. This is about spiritual perception—the ability to sense, discern, and understand what's happening in the unseen realm.

Most people are born with this ability. Children naturally sense atmospheres, feel when something is wrong, and recognize when people carry darkness. But over time, layer by layer, the soul develops curtains that block spiritual sight.

These curtains aren't accidental. They're carefully constructed through:

- Conditioning that teaches you to ignore your instincts
- Trauma that makes you distrust your discernment
- Religion that replaces relationship with ritual
- Culture that mocks spiritual sensitivity
- Fear that paralyzes you from acting on what you sense

By adulthood, most people are spiritually blind—walking through a world filled with invisible activity while seeing none of it.

The soul can be blindfolded without the person ever realizing they've lost their sight.

Stage 1: Dismissal in Childhood

It starts early. A child senses something wrong and is told, 'There's nothing there.' A child feels afraid of a person and is told, 'Don't be rude.' A child refuses to enter a space and is told, 'Stop being dramatic.'

Over time, the child learns to override their discernment. They learn that what they sense isn't real, isn't valid, isn't worth paying attention to.

The first curtain drops.

Stage 2: Rationalization in Adolescence

By the teenage years, the curtains thicken. Spiritual sensitivity is replaced with logic, reason, and the need to fit in. Anything that can't be explained scientifically is dismissed as superstition or imagination.

The person begins to rationalize away every spiritual warning:

- 'I'm just overthinking.'

* 'It's probably nothing.'
* 'I'm being paranoid.'
* 'There's a logical explanation.'

The second curtain drops.

Stage 3: Trauma-Induced Shutdown

When someone experiences spiritual trauma—betrayal, abuse, oppression, or attack—without understanding what happened to them, they often shut down entirely.

They stop trusting their instincts. They stop believing what they sense. They convince themselves they're broken, crazy, or cursed.

And so they close off their spiritual senses completely as a form of self-protection.

The third curtain drops.

Stage 4: Religious Programming

For many believers, the final curtain comes from religion itself. They're taught formulas instead of relationship. Rules instead of discernment. Routine instead of revelation.

They're told when to pray, what to say, how to behave—but they're never taught how to hear God's voice, sense spiritual atmospheres, or recognize demonic interference.

Spirituality becomes performance. Faith becomes compliance. And the soul becomes completely blindfolded.

The fourth curtain drops.

What Happens When the Soul Is Blindfolded

When you can't see the unseen realm, you become vulnerable to:

- Spiritual attacks you don't recognize
- Demonic assignments you can't identify
- Toxic relationships you don't discern
- Contaminated atmospheres you absorb without awareness
- Manipulation you mistake for leadership
- Oppression you accept as normal life

You blame yourself for problems that aren't yours. You fight battles in the natural realm that are rooted in the spiritual. You exhaust yourself trying to fix what only God can reveal and remove.

And worst of all—you never realize you're blind. Because when the curtains drop slowly enough, you don't notice the darkness.

The most dangerous blindness is the blindness you don't know you have.

The good news is this: What has been blindfolded can be unveiled. What has been muted can be restored. What has been shut down can be reactivated.

But it requires:

1. Acknowledgment

You have to acknowledge that you've been blind. That you've been ignoring your discernment. That you've been rationalizing away spiritual warnings.

Until you admit the curtains are there, they'll stay there.

2. Repentance

Repentance means changing direction. It means choosing to trust your spiritual senses again instead of dismissing them. It means asking God to restore what you've shut down.

3. Retraining

Your spiritual senses are like muscles. If they haven't been used in years, they need to be strengthened. You retrain them by:

- Paying attention to what you sense
- Trusting your discernment even when you can't explain it
- Acting on spiritual warnings instead of ignoring them
- Asking God for wisdom and clarity

4. Community

You need people around you who understand spiritual warfare and can help you interpret what you're sensing. People who won't dismiss your discernment or call you paranoid.

The enemy isolates. God connects.

When the curtains are removed and your spiritual sight is restored, everything changes.

You walk into rooms differently. You engage with people differently. You make decisions differently.

Because you're no longer reacting to what you see—you're responding to what you sense.

And that makes all the difference.

SECTION II
UNDERSTANDING SPIRITUAL WARFARE

Most people think spiritual warfare looks like dramatic confrontations with demons.

But the reality is far more subtle—and far more dangerous.

True spiritual warfare happens in the everyday: in conversations, relationships, workplaces, homes. It moves through personalities, patterns, and atmospheres.

This section will teach you to recognize the true nature of warfare and the enemy's most common tactics.

CHAPTER 5

When most people think of spiritual warfare, they imagine exorcisms, demons manifesting, and dramatic spiritual battles.

But that's Hollywood. That's not how the enemy actually operates most of the time.

The true nature of warfare is not horror-movie demons. It's people, placements, and patterns.

Let me explain what that means.

Warfare Through People

The enemy rarely attacks you directly. He uses people.

Not necessarily evil people. Not people with horns and pitchforks. Just regular people who—knowingly or unknowingly—carry spiritual assignments against you.

These people can be:

- Coworkers who undermine you
- Family members who plant doubt

- Friends who drain your energy
- Mentors who redirect your destiny
- Strangers who appear at critical moments

Most of them don't even know they're being used. They think they're just following their instincts, expressing their opinions, or acting on their feelings.

But behind those instincts, opinions, and feelings? There's often a spirit at work.

This is why you can't fight spiritual warfare by fighting people. You have to recognize what's operating through them and address it at the spiritual level.

Warfare Through Placements

The enemy is strategic. He doesn't just attack randomly—he positions people and circumstances precisely to interfere with your assignment.

Placements include:

- The roommate who moved in right before your breakthrough
- The supervisor who was assigned to your department weeks before your promotion
- The person who keeps appearing wherever you go
- The opportunity that came at exactly the wrong time

These aren't coincidences. These are placements.

The enemy studies you. He knows your patterns, your weaknesses, your triggers. And he positions people and circumstances to exploit them.

Once you start recognizing placements, you'll see them everywhere. And you'll stop being surprised when opposition shows up right before breakthroughs.

Warfare Through Patterns

One of the enemy's most effective tactics is repetition. He creates patterns that keep you trapped in cycles you can't seem to break.

Patterns like:

- Relationships that always end the same way
- Jobs that always become toxic after a certain amount of time
- Breakthroughs that always get sabotaged at the last minute
- Health issues that flare up during significant seasons
- Financial setbacks that happen right before increase

These patterns aren't just bad luck. They're spiritual assignments designed to keep you stuck, discouraged, and defeated.

Breaking patterns requires recognizing them first. Once you see the pattern, you can interrupt it spiritually through prayer, deliverance, and strategic action.

Understanding the true nature of warfare changes everything.

You stop blaming yourself for things that aren't your fault. You stop fighting people when the real enemy is spiritual. You stop accepting patterns as 'just how life is.'

Instead, you start seeing clearly. You recognize assignments. You discern placements. You break patterns.

And you walk in the authority God gave you to overcome.

CHAPTER 6

The Enemy's Most Common Tactics

The enemy doesn't have unlimited strategies. He uses the same tactics over and over because they work.

Once you recognize these tactics, you'll see them operating everywhere—in your workplace, your relationships, your family, your church.

Here are the seven most common:

1. Jealousy

Jealousy is one of the enemy's favorite tools. It turns people against you without them even understanding why.

Someone sees your favor, your anointing, your opportunities—and something rises up in them. They don't celebrate you. They compete with you. They undermine you. They work against you.

And often, they don't even realize they're being driven by jealousy. They rationalize it as 'fairness' or 'concern' or 'accountability.'

But at the root? It's jealousy.

Jealousy:

- Makes people sabotage what they can't control
- Turns allies into opponents
- Blocks blessings that should flow freely
- Creates division where there should be unity

2. Envy

Envy is jealousy's twin, but it goes deeper. Jealousy wants what you have. Envy wants to BE you.

Envy doesn't just compete—it covets your identity, your calling, your essence.

People operating in envy:

- Study how you move and try to replicate it
- Mimic your style, your voice, your methods
- Position themselves near you to absorb your influence
- Become spiritually invasive without crossing physical boundaries

3. Mimicry

This is one of the most overlooked tactics—and one of the most dangerous.

Spirits of mimicry operate through people who copy you, mirror you, and attach themselves to your identity in ways that feel invasive even though you can't explain why.

They don't just admire you. They study you. They track your patterns. They adopt your mannerisms, your language, your decisions.

And it's not innocent. It's spiritual identity theft.

(We'll explore this in depth in Chapter 7.)

4. Siphoning

Some people drain you. Not because they're needy—because they're spiritually extracting from you.

Siphoning is the act of pulling energy, strength, creativity, or anointing from someone without their awareness.

After being around these people, you feel:

- Exhausted even though the conversation was brief
- Empty even though nothing dramatic happened
- Depleted even though you gave nothing tangible

That's siphoning.

The enemy loves to wear you out. Not through visible attacks, but through relentless, low-grade spiritual exhaustion.

This fatigue:

- Makes you too tired to pray
- Clouds your ability to think clearly
- Weakens your resistance to temptation
- Makes everything feel harder than it should be

Spiritual fatigue is designed to make you quit before you finish.

Confusion is a spirit. It's not you being indecisive or unclear—it's an assignment designed to cloud your mind right when you need clarity most.

Confusion shows up:

- Right before major decisions
- During critical transitions
- When you're close to breakthrough
- In relationships that should be clear

Where the Spirit of God is, there is clarity. Where confusion persists, there's interference.

The enemy knows you're stronger in community. So he isolates you.

He makes you feel:

- Misunderstood
- Alone
- Like no one gets you
- Like you're better off by yourself

And slowly, he cuts you off from the people who could strengthen, support, and sharpen you.

Isolation makes you vulnerable. It makes you paranoid. It makes you weak.

If the enemy can isolate you, he can defeat you.

Now that you know these seven tactics, start watching for them:

- Is someone operating in jealousy toward you?
- Do you feel siphoned around certain people?
- Is confusion clouding decisions that should be clear?
- Are you being isolated from your support system?

Once you recognize the tactic, you can respond strategically instead of reacting emotionally.

And that changes everything.

SESSION 3

Chapters 7-9

Section II Conclusion & Section III Begins

There is a spiritual phenomenon that most people never recognize, even when they're experiencing it firsthand.

It's called mimicry—and it's one of the most invasive, subtle, and damaging forms of spiritual warfare.

> **Mimicry is not admiration. It's spiritual identity theft.**

Let me explain.

What Is the Spirit of Mimicry?

The spirit of mimicry operates through people who don't just admire you—they study you, copy you, and attach themselves to your identity in ways that feel invasive even though you can't explain why.

They mimic:

- Your speech patterns and phrases
- Your mannerisms and expressions
- Your style and aesthetic choices
- Your goals and life decisions

- Your relationships and connections
- Your spiritual language and revelation

At first, it looks like flattery. It looks like someone who admires you and wants to be like you.

But there's a difference between admiration and mimicry:

Admiration celebrates you. Mimicry copies you.

Admiration learns from you. Mimicry extracts from you.

Admiration honors your uniqueness. Mimicry tries to replace you.

How Mimicry Operates

People operating in mimicry don't usually know they're doing it. They genuinely believe they're just 'relating to you' or 'being inspired by you.'

But what's actually happening is far more insidious.

Mimicry operates in stages:

Stage 1: Observation

They watch you closely. They study how you move, how you speak, how you carry yourself. They pay attention to details others might miss.

Stage 2: Replication

They begin copying you—sometimes subtly, sometimes blatantly. They adopt your phrases, your style, your methods. They position themselves in similar spaces, pursue similar opportunities, even connect with similar people.

Stage 3: Invasion

They cross boundaries that feel intangible but very real. You start feeling like they're too close, too similar, too attached to your identity.

You can't point to anything concrete. But your spirit knows something is wrong.

Stage 4: Replacement

This is the goal of mimicry—to become you or replace you in spaces where you're supposed to operate.

They position themselves as 'just as good,' 'just as anointed,' 'just as capable.' And because they've studied you so closely, they can sometimes pull it off—at least on the surface.

Mimicry is dangerous because:

- It's spiritually invasive—violating boundaries you can feel but can't see
- It drains your energy—you feel depleted being around them
- It confuses your identity—when someone mirrors you too closely, it can make you question yourself
- It redirects your influence—they siphon favor, connections, and opportunities that were meant for you
- It's hard to address—because it looks innocent on the surface

Most people who experience mimicry don't know how to respond. They feel crazy for being bothered by it. They feel guilty for setting boundaries. They feel selfish for wanting space.

But your discomfort is valid. Your discernment is accurate. And your boundaries are necessary.

Real-Life Example: The Individual Pattern

In the source material for this book, there's reference to 'Individual'—a person who operated in textbook mimicry.

This person:

- Watched closely and copied patterns
- Positioned themselves in proximity repeatedly
- Mirrored decisions and directions
- Created an atmosphere of spiritual invasion
- Left the person feeling monitored, not admired

And here's the key: Individual likely didn't know they were operating in mimicry. They probably thought they were just 'connecting' or 'relating.'

But the spirit behind it? That spirit knew exactly what it was doing.

1. Trust Your Discernment

If someone feels invasive, trust that. You don't need proof. You don't need to explain it. Your discernment is enough.

2. Create Distance

You don't owe mimics proximity. Create space. Limit access. Protect your energy.

3. Guard Your Revelation

Stop sharing your visions, dreams, strategies, and downloads with people who copy instead of celebrate you.

4. Pray for Release

Mimicry is a spiritual attachment. Pray for God to sever the connection and release you from the invasion.

5. Don't Explain Yourself

You don't have to justify your boundaries to people who won't understand them. Move quietly. Protect yourself wisely.

Mimicry thrives in proximity. Distance weakens it. Boundaries break it.

CHAPTER 8

Strongholds, Bondage, and Soul Dulling

Not all spiritual warfare is external. Some of the fiercest battles happen inside—within your own mind, emotions, and will.

These internal battles are called strongholds.

A stronghold is a pattern of thinking that gives the enemy legal ground to operate in your life.

What Is a Stronghold?

A stronghold is a fortified place in your mind where the enemy has established a base of operations.

It's built through:

- Repeated lies you've believed
- Trauma you haven't healed from
- Sin you've normalized
- Agreements you've made with darkness

Once a stronghold is established, it influences everything:

- How you think
- How you feel

- What you believe about yourself
- What you believe about God
- What decisions you make

Common strongholds include:

- Fear and anxiety
- Shame and guilt
- Rejection and abandonment
- Worthlessness and self-hatred
- Anger and bitterness
- Addiction and bondage

How Strongholds Form

Strongholds don't appear overnight. They're built brick by brick, thought by thought.

Here's how it happens:

Step 1: A Lie Is Introduced

The enemy whispers a lie: 'You're not good enough.' 'God doesn't love you.' 'You'll never change.' 'You deserve this pain.'

Step 2: The Lie Is Believed

Instead of rejecting the lie, you agree with it. You accept it as truth.

Step 3: The Lie Is Repeated

The more you think it, the stronger it gets. Repetition builds the walls of the stronghold.

Step 4: The Lie Becomes a Filter

Eventually, the lie becomes the lens through which you interpret everything. It colors your thoughts, shapes your emotions, and controls your behavior.

Step 5: The Stronghold Is Fortified

Now the enemy doesn't even have to attack you from outside. The stronghold does his work for him from within.

What Is Bondage?

Bondage is when a stronghold has progressed to the point where you feel powerless to break free.

You know something is wrong. You want to change. But you can't seem to break the pattern.

Bondage can manifest as:

- Addiction you can't overcome
- Thought patterns you can't escape
- Emotions that control you
- Behaviors you can't stop

Bondage makes you feel trapped, hopeless, and defeated.

But here's the truth: You're not powerless. You're bound. And what's bound can be loosed.

Soul Dulling: When the Enemy Numbs You

Soul dulling is what happens when the enemy can't destroy you outright—so he settles for making you numb.

A dulled soul:

- Feels nothing deeply
- Cares about nothing passionately
- Pursues nothing purposefully
- Lives on autopilot

Soul dulling is dangerous because it's subtle. You don't realize it's happening until you wake up one day and realize you don't feel alive anymore.

You're just... existing.

1. Identify the Lie

What lie have you been believing? What thought pattern keeps repeating?

2. Renounce the Lie

Out loud, reject it. Say, 'I renounce the lie that [insert lie]. I refuse to agree with it any longer.'

3. Replace With Truth

Find scripture that speaks truth over the lie. Meditate on it. Declare it. Let God's Word become your new filter.

4. Seek Deliverance If Needed

Some strongholds require deliverance ministry. Don't be afraid to ask for help.

5. Guard Your Mind

Don't let the lie back in. Monitor what you think, what you watch, what you listen to.

Breaking strongholds is not about willpower. It's about truth displacing lies.

SECTION III
DISCERNMENT ESSENTIALS

Discernment is not paranoia. It's not suspicion. It's not overthinking.

Discernment is spiritual intelligence—the ability to perceive, interpret, and respond to the unseen realm with wisdom and clarity.

This section will teach you to recognize spiritual gatekeepers, identify parasitic relationships, develop your discernment gift, and understand how access points work.

CHAPTER 9

Spiritual Gatekeepers

A gatekeeper is someone who controls access.

In the natural realm, gatekeepers decide who gets in, who gets promoted, who gets opportunities, and who gets blocked.

In the spiritual realm, gatekeepers operate the same way—but their control is far more insidious because it's invisible.

Spiritual gatekeepers are people positioned to block access, sabotage destiny, or run the atmosphere.

What Spiritual Gatekeepers Do

Spiritual gatekeepers:

- Block opportunities that should be yours
- Sabotage relationships that would advance you
- Control atmospheres to keep you suppressed
- Monitor your moves and report to darkness
- Redirect your destiny through subtle influence

They don't do this overtly. They do it through:

- Seemingly innocent questions that gather intel
- Advice that sounds wise but redirects you
- Influence that positions them between you and your breakthrough
- Presence that shifts atmospheres whenever you're about to advance

How to Recognize Spiritual Gatekeepers

Gatekeepers often appear helpful, supportive, even mentoring. But pay attention to patterns:

- Opportunities close when they're involved
- Your peace leaves in their presence
- They position themselves at critical junctures
- They ask invasive questions disguised as concern
- They control who you have access to
- You feel monitored, not mentored

How to Respond

Don't confront gatekeepers directly—they'll deny it, gaslight you, or turn it back on you.

Instead:

- Limit their access to information about your plans
- Create distance strategically
- Pray for God to remove or neutralize their influence

- Move when God says move—don't wait for their approval

Gatekeepers only have the power you give them. Reclaim your authority.

SESSION 4

Chapters 10-12

Completing Section III - Discernment Essentials

CHAPTER 10

Some relationships drain you. Not because they're difficult—because they're parasitic.

A parasite is an organism that lives off another organism, taking without giving, draining without replenishing.

In the spiritual realm, parasites operate the same way.

Spiritual parasites are people who attach to you, extract from you, and weaken you—all while appearing normal on the surface.

What Are Spiritual Parasites?

Spiritual parasites are people who:

- Drain your energy consistently
- Take your time, attention, and resources without reciprocating
- Leave you feeling depleted after every interaction
- Attach to you in ways that feel invasive
- Feed off your anointing, favor, or strength

They're not necessarily bad people. They're not always intentionally harmful. But they're spiritually extractive.

And the longer they stay attached, the weaker you become.

What Are Spiritual Vampires?

Spiritual vampires are similar to parasites, but more aggressive. They don't just passively drain—they actively siphon.

Vampires:

- Seek you out when they need something
- Extract your energy, ideas, or anointing
- Leave you feeling hollow after encounters
- Return repeatedly to feed
- Show no awareness of what they're taking

You'll notice that after being around them, you feel:

- Exhausted for no logical reason
- Emotionally depleted
- Spiritually flat
- Like something was taken from you

That's because something was.

How to Recognize Parasites and Vampires

Pay attention to these signs:

1. You Feel Drained After Every Interaction

Even brief conversations leave you exhausted. Even text exchanges feel draining.

2. They Only Appear When They Need Something

They disappear when you need support but show up when they need help, advice, prayer, or resources.

3. The Relationship Is One-Sided

You pour in. They take. You give. They receive. There's no reciprocity.

4. You Can't Seem to Distance Yourself

Even when you try to create space, they find ways to re-attach. They guilt you, manipulate you, or just show up uninvited.

5. Your Peace Drops Around Them

You lose your sense of calm, clarity, and strength in their presence.

These relationships are dangerous because:

- They weaken you slowly over time
- They normalize energy extraction
- They make you feel guilty for setting boundaries
- They can attach spiritually in ways that persist even after physical separation

If left unchecked, parasitic relationships will drain you to the point where you have nothing left to give—not even to yourself.

1. Recognize the Pattern

Acknowledge that the relationship is extractive. Stop rationalizing it.

2. Set Firm Boundaries

Limit access. Reduce availability. Don't feel guilty about protecting your energy.

3. Pray for Spiritual Severance

Ask God to cut the spiritual attachment. Some connections require supernatural intervention.

4. Don't Explain Yourself

Parasites and vampires will never understand your boundaries. Stop trying to make them.

5. Replenish What Was Taken

After breaking free, focus on restoration. Rest. Pray. Spend time in God's presence. Let Him restore what was drained.

You are not responsible for feeding everyone who's spiritually hungry. Protect your energy.

CHAPTER 11

The Gift of Discernment

Discernment is one of the most misunderstood gifts in the Body of Christ.

People think it's:

- Being judgmental
- Being suspicious of everyone
- Having a critical spirit
- Finding fault in everything

But that's not discernment. That's dysfunction.

Discernment is the spiritual ability to perceive what's really happening beyond what's visible.

What Discernment Is—and Isn't

Discernment IS:

- Spiritual intelligence
- The ability to sense atmospheres
- Recognizing spirits operating through people
- Perceiving hidden motives and agendas
- Knowing when something is off even without proof

Discernment IS NOT:

- Suspicion
- Paranoia
- Assuming the worst about everyone
- Using your 'gift' to criticize and judge

True discernment doesn't make you harsh—it makes you wise.

Discernment operates through:

1. Your Spirit

You sense things before you think them. You know before you understand. This is your spirit picking up on spiritual activity.

2. Your Body

Physical reactions—tension, discomfort, unease—are often your body responding to spiritual danger.

3. Your Peace

When peace leaves, God is speaking. When peace stays, you're in alignment.

4. Your Dreams

God often reveals through dreams what He can't get through during waking hours.

Discernment is sharpened through:

1. Paying Attention

Notice what you sense. Don't dismiss it. Don't rationalize it. Just notice.

2. Trusting Yourself

Stop second-guessing your discernment. If something feels off, it probably is.

3. Testing What You Sense

Watch and see if your discernment proves accurate. Over time, you'll learn to trust it more.

4. Asking God for Clarity

Discernment without wisdom can be dangerous. Always ask God to clarify what you're sensing and show you how to respond.

1. Using It to Gossip

Discernment is not a license to expose everyone. Handle what God reveals with wisdom and discretion.

2. Becoming Paranoid

Discernment should bring clarity, not constant anxiety. If you're constantly suspicious of everyone, that's not discernment—that's trauma or fear.

3. Ignoring It

The worst thing you can do with discernment is override it. When God warns you, listen.

Discernment is God's gift to protect you. Honor it by using it wisely.

CHAPTER 12

Open Doors and Forced Doors

Not every open door is from God. And not every closed door is from the enemy.

One of the most critical skills in spiritual warfare is learning to discern the difference between:

- Doors God opens
- Doors you force open
- Doors the enemy opens
- Doors God closes for your protection

Access is not the same as assignment. Just because you can enter doesn't mean you should.

How Spirits Get Access

The enemy operates through access points—spiritual doors that grant him legal permission to influence your life.

These doors include:

1. Sin

Ongoing, unrepentant sin creates legal ground for the enemy. The longer the sin continues, the stronger the access.

2. Trauma

Unhealed wounds become entry points for tormenting spirits. If you don't let God heal it, the enemy will exploit it.

3. Agreements

When you believe lies—'I'm worthless,' 'God doesn't love me,' 'I'll never change'—you create agreements with darkness.

4. Unforgiveness

Holding onto bitterness binds you to the person who hurt you and gives the enemy access to both of you.

5. Soul Ties

Sexual sin, deep emotional bonds, or covenants create spiritual connections that transfer influence.

6. Occult Involvement

Even 'innocent' participation—horoscopes, tarot, witchcraft, séances—opens demonic doors.

Sometimes we force doors open that God wanted closed. And sometimes we resist doors God is opening.

Here's how to tell the difference:

God-Opened Doors:

- Align with His Word and His character
- Come with peace, even if there's fear
- Don't require manipulation or compromise
- Are confirmed through multiple sources
- Feel right in your spirit

Forced Doors:

- Require you to compromise your values
- Come with constant anxiety or unease
- Demand that you manipulate circumstances
- Lack confirmation or peace
- Feel wrong even though they look good

1. Identify the Access Point

Ask God to reveal what door the enemy is using. Be honest about sin, trauma, or agreements.

2. Repent

If sin opened the door, repentance closes it. Don't just feel bad—turn away from it.

3. Renounce Agreements

Out loud, reject lies you've believed. Break agreements with darkness.

4. Forgive

Release people who hurt you. Unforgiveness keeps doors open.

5. Seek Deliverance if Needed

Some doors require deliverance ministry to fully close. Don't be afraid to ask for help.

The enemy can only operate where you give him access. Close the doors.

In the next section, we'll explore how prayer shifts atmospheres and how to walk in your spiritual authority.

SESSION 5

Chapters 13-16 + Conclusion

Section IV: Prayer, Authority, and Awakening

Final Session - Completing Volume A

SECTION IV
PRAYER, AUTHORITY, AND AWAKENING

Understanding the unseen realm is only the first step.

The next step is learning how to operate in it with power and authority.

This final section teaches you how to shift atmospheres through prayer, recognize angelic assistance, walk in your spiritual identity, and maintain deliverance.

CHAPTER 13

How Prayer Shifts Atmospheres

Prayer is not just talking to God. Prayer is spiritual warfare.

When you pray, you're not just expressing your needs—you're shifting atmospheres, breaking assignments, and releasing heaven's influence into earthly situations.

> **Prayer doesn't just ask God to intervene. Prayer creates the conditions for intervention to manifest.**

Why Prayer Works

Prayer works because it:

- Invites God's presence into contaminated spaces
- Breaks demonic assignments
- Activates angelic activity
- Aligns the natural realm with heaven's will
- Establishes your authority as a believer

When you pray, you're not begging God to do something. You're partnering with Him to manifest what's already been decreed in heaven.

There's a difference between praying out of emotion and praying strategically.

Emotional Prayer:

- Reacts to what you feel
- Changes based on circumstances
- Can be desperate or frantic
- Lacks focus and direction

Strategic Prayer:

- Responds to what God reveals
- Remains steady regardless of circumstances
- Is focused and authoritative
- Targets specific assignments and atmospheres

Both are valid. But strategic prayer is what shifts atmospheres.

1. Discern What Needs to Shift

Before you pray, ask God what you're dealing with. Is it oppression? Confusion? A demonic assignment? An ungodly atmosphere?

2. Pray With Authority, Not Desperation

You have authority in Christ. Command atmospheres to shift.
Declare God's will. Don't beg—declare.

3. Be Specific

General prayers get general results. Specific prayers break
specific assignments.

4. Pray Consistently

Some atmospheres require sustained prayer before they break.
Don't give up after one prayer.

5. Watch for the Shift

You'll know when the atmosphere shifts. The heaviness lifts.
Peace returns. Clarity comes.

**Prayer is your primary weapon in spiritual warfare.
Use it strategically.**

CHAPTER 14

Angels and Invisible Reinforcements

You are not alone in spiritual warfare.

God has assigned angels to assist you, protect you, and execute His will on your behalf.

Most believers have no idea how active angels are in their lives. They assume angels only show up in dramatic biblical moments— burning bushes, empty tombs, angelic visitations.

But angels are constantly at work in the unseen realm, responding to prayers, protecting from attacks, and enforcing heaven's decrees.

> **Angels are not symbolic. They are real, active, and assigned.**

What Angels Do

According to Scripture, angels:

- Minister to believers (Hebrews 1:14)
- Guard and protect (Psalm 91:11)
- Execute God's judgments (2 Kings 19:35)
- Deliver messages (Luke 1:26-38)

- Battle demonic forces (Daniel 10:13)
- Respond to prayer and worship (Revelation 8:3-4)

They are warriors, messengers, protectors, and enforcers of God's will.

You don't pray to angels—you pray to God, and angels respond.

But you can activate angelic assistance by:

1. Speaking God's Word

Angels respond to God's Word. When you declare Scripture, you give angels legal ground to act.

2. Worshiping

Worship shifts atmospheres and activates angelic presence.

3. Praying in Alignment With Heaven

When your prayers align with God's will, angels move to enforce
what you've declared.

4. Walking in Obedience

Obedience grants angels access. Disobedience limits their ability
to assist you.

**You're not fighting alone. Heaven's reinforcements
are already assigned.**

CHAPTER 15

Your Spiritual Identity & Authority

The enemy's primary goal is not to destroy you—it's to make you forget who you are.

If he can keep you from understanding your spiritual identity and authority, he doesn't have to fight you. You'll fight yourself.

You are not a victim of spiritual warfare. You are a warrior with authority.

Who You Are in Christ

Your identity is not based on your performance, your past, or your feelings. It's based on what Christ accomplished.

In Christ, you are:

- A child of God (John 1:12)
- Seated in heavenly places (Ephesians 2:6)
- More than a conqueror (Romans 8:37)
- The righteousness of God (2 Corinthians 5:21)
- Given authority over the enemy (Luke 10:19)

This is not theology. This is your reality.

Authority is delegated power. You don't have it because you earned it—you have it because Christ gave it to you.

Your authority allows you to:

- Bind and loose (Matthew 18:18)
- Cast out demons (Mark 16:17)
- Trample serpents and scorpions (Luke 10:19)
- Resist the devil (James 4:7)
- Shift atmospheres (Ephesians 6:12)

But authority unused is authority wasted.

1. Know Who You Are

You can't walk in authority you don't believe you have. Study your identity in Christ.

2. Speak With Confidence

Your words carry weight in the spiritual realm. Speak truth, declare God's Word, command atmospheres to shift.

3. Don't Tolerate Oppression

You have authority to resist. Stop accepting what you have the power to reject.

4. Live From Your Identity

Don't let circumstances, people, or attacks define you. Let Christ define you.

The enemy can only operate where you allow him. Reclaim your authority.

CHAPTER 16

Deliverance and Reinforcement

Deliverance is not a one-time event. It's an ongoing process of staying spiritually clean.

You can experience breakthrough, break free from bondage, and close demonic doors—but if you don't maintain that freedom, the enemy will return.

Freedom requires maintenance. Deliverance requires reinforcement.

What Is Deliverance?

Deliverance is the process of breaking free from demonic oppression, strongholds, and bondage.

It involves:

- Identifying what's binding you
- Repenting of access points
- Renouncing agreements with darkness
- Commanding spirits to leave
- Closing doors they've been using

1. Guard What You Consume

What you watch, listen to, and read affects your spiritual state. Choose wisely.

2. Stay in God's Presence

Regular prayer, worship, and time in the Word keep you spiritually strong.

3. Maintain Boundaries

Don't let toxic people, contaminated atmospheres, or ungodly relationships back in.

4. Address Issues Quickly

When you sense oppression returning, deal with it immediately. Don't let it take root.

5. Walk in Community

You need people who can pray with you, encourage you, and hold you accountable.

Deliverance is not the end. It's the beginning of walking in sustained freedom.

CONCLUSION

You've reached the end of Volume A: Foundations.

But this is not the end of your journey. This is the beginning.

You now have language for what you've been experiencing. You have a framework for understanding the unseen realm. You have tools for recognizing spiritual warfare and responding with wisdom.

But knowledge alone won't protect you. You must apply what you've learned.

What Comes Next

Keep this book close. Return to it when:

- You walk into an atmosphere that feels off
- You encounter a person who drains you
- You experience unexplained oppression
- You need to shift an atmosphere through prayer
- You're in a season of spiritual attack

This book is a reference, not just a read. Use it. Mark it up. Return to it.

Volume B: Advanced Assignments

Volume A has given you the foundations. Volume B will take you deeper.

In Volume B, you'll learn:

- Advanced spiritual structures and shadow hierarchies
- Coordinated opposition and hidden networks
- Warfare over men and women specifically
- Workplace and institutional spiritual warfare
- Advanced protection strategies
- How to become spiritually unshakeable

But before you move to Volume B, master what's in Volume A. Let these foundations become second nature.

Final Words

The unseen realm is real. You're not imagining it. You're not paranoid. You're not crazy.

You're awake.

And now that you're awake, you can never go back to living blind.

Walk in authority. Move in wisdom. Live in freedom.

May your eyes remain open.

May your discernment sharpen.

May your peace return.

May your authority activate.

And may nothing unseen ever surprise you again.

— Tavaca Dorsey

For we wrestle not against flesh and blood,

but against principalities, against powers,

against the rulers of the darkness of this world,

against spiritual wickedness in high places.

— Ephesians 6:12 (KJV)

ABOUT THE AUTHOR

Tavaca Dorsey is a faith-led author and emerging voice in spiritual clarity, discernment, and identity restoration. She was not trained in a classroom, mentored by institutions, or coached into awareness. Her wisdom was forged through a lived, holy wilderness experience in the desert heat of Kuwait, where the unseen realm became undeniable and language finally met reality.

She writes from revelation, not theory—translating invisible spiritual dynamics into words that everyday people can finally recognize, understand, and apply.

Her mission is simple:

- To help others see what they were never taught to see
- To reclaim what was quietly warred against
- To walk in authority with understanding, not fear

Tavaca's work reaches those who always sensed something deeper, those who lived through invisible warfare without vocabulary, and those ready to break cycles by gaining spiritual intelligence. She is committed to equipping readers, not impressing them—because clarity rescues lives, destinies, and identities.

She writes for those who are awakening.

VOLUME B

ADVANCED ASSIGNMENTS

VOLUME B INTRODUCTION

Moving Beyond Foundations

If Volume A gave you eyes to see the unseen realm, Volume B will teach you how to operate in it with precision.

This is not beginner material. This is advanced spiritual warfare for those who've already awakened and are ready to go deeper.

In Volume B, you will learn:

- How spiritual structures and shadow hierarchies operate
- Coordinated opposition and hidden spiritual networks
- Gender-specific warfare tactics against men and women
- Workplace and institutional spiritual dynamics
- Advanced protection strategies
- How to become spiritually unshakeable

This volume is for those who are serious about spiritual warfare—not curious, but committed.

Let's begin.

SECTION V
ADVANCED SPIRITUAL STRUCTURES

The enemy doesn't operate randomly. He operates through structures, hierarchies, and coordinated systems.

Understanding these structures is essential for advanced spiritual warfare.

CHAPTER 17

Shadow Hierarchies and Spiritual Networks

In the unseen realm, there are hierarchies—organized structures of demonic authority.

These aren't random demons floating around. They're organized, strategic, and assigned.

The enemy operates through rank, order, and delegated authority—just like heaven does.

Understanding Spiritual Rank

Scripture reveals spiritual hierarchy:

- Principalities - territorial rulers over regions
- Powers - authorities over specific domains
- Rulers of darkness - governors of systems
- Spiritual wickedness in high places - coordinators of evil

Each rank has specific assignments, territories, and methods of operation.

How Shadow Networks Operate

Shadow networks are invisible connections between people who share similar assignments, even if they don't know each other.

You'll notice:

- People appearing in coordinated patterns
- Opposition intensifying from multiple sources simultaneously
- Information spreading through channels you can't trace
- Resistance showing up in unrelated areas at the same time

This isn't coincidence. It's coordination.

Recognizing Coordinated Attacks

Coordinated attacks manifest as:

- Multiple people opposing you at once
- Problems erupting in different areas simultaneously
- Resources being blocked from multiple directions
- Sudden isolation from support systems

When attacks coordinate, you're dealing with hierarchical assignment, not random opposition.

Coordinated attacks require coordinated prayer and strategic spiritual response.

CHAPTER 18

Territorial Spirits and Environmental Warfare

Not all warfare is personal.

Some warfare is territorial.

There are spiritual forces assigned not just to people, but to regions, cities, buildings, institutions, and environments. These forces influence what happens within their assigned territory. They shape atmosphere, behavior, perception, and resistance to truth.

Territorial spirits operate by legal access and sustained presence.

They do not appear randomly. They are assigned.

Scripture reveals this structure clearly. In Daniel 10, the angel sent to deliver Daniel's answer was delayed by the "Prince of Persia"—a territorial spiritual authority governing that region. This was not symbolic language. It was a direct revelation of organized spiritual jurisdiction.

This confirms that spiritual warfare exists not only on the individual level, but on the environmental level.

Some environments carry resistance.

Some environments carry heaviness.

Some environments carry confusion, stagnation, oppression, or hostility.

These are not always psychological or emotional conditions. They are often manifestations of sustained spiritual presence.

Atmosphere Is Not Neutral

Every environment carries an atmosphere.

Atmosphere is the spiritual climate created by whatever authority has been operating there consistently.

Just as natural climates form over time through repeated weather patterns, spiritual climates form through repeated spiritual activity.

Where darkness has operated unchecked, the atmosphere becomes heavy.

Where fear has been sustained, the atmosphere becomes restrictive.

Where truth has been suppressed, the atmosphere becomes resistant to revelation.

Atmosphere influences perception, behavior, and response.

People entering these environments often experience shifts in clarity, energy, confidence, or peace without understanding why.

This is environmental warfare.

Territorial Spirits Establish Influence Through Access Points

Territorial spirits gain and maintain influence through access points.

These access points include:

• Persistent sin
• Agreement with deception
• Trauma and unhealed wounds
• Idolatry
• Fear
• Repeated spiritual compromise
• Covenants made knowingly or unknowingly

Over time, these access points create legal permission for sustained spiritual occupation.

This occupation affects individuals living, working, or operating within that territory.

It can influence decision-making, emotional stability, relationships, and spiritual sensitivity.

This influence is subtle but strategic.

It seeks to normalize dysfunction.

It seeks to suppress awareness.

It seeks to prevent resistance.

Not Every Battle Originates Within You

One of the most important revelations is this:

Not every struggle originates within you.

Some resistance is environmental.

Some heaviness is atmospheric.

Some opposition is territorial.

Without this understanding, individuals may misinterpret environmental warfare as personal weakness, failure, or instability.

This creates unnecessary self-condemnation.

The enemy benefits when territorial warfare is mistaken for personal deficiency.

Discernment removes false self-blame.

Discernment reveals the true source.

Once the source is revealed, authority can be applied correctly.

Authority Disrupts Territorial Influence

Territorial spirits maintain influence through consistency.

They lose influence through disruption.

Authority disrupts their operations.

Prayer shifts atmosphere.

Truth weakens deception.

Light exposes hidden activity.

Agreement with divine authority overrides unauthorized spiritual occupation.

Presence matters.

When an individual operating in spiritual authority enters an environment, the atmosphere begins to shift.

Resistance may increase temporarily.

This is not defeat.

This is exposure.

Darkness resists exposure because exposure precedes displacement.

You Were Not Sent Without Authority

You were not placed in your environment randomly.

Assignment and placement are not accidents.

Where you are positioned, you carry authority to influence.

Not through force.

Not through confrontation.

But through alignment, presence, and obedience.

Authority does not require announcement.

Authority requires alignment.

When aligned, your presence alone disrupts unauthorized spiritual activity.

Peace becomes established where unrest once dominated.

Clarity emerges where confusion once operated.

Light occupies where darkness once functioned undetected.

This is not personal power.

This is delegated authority.

Territorial warfare is not overcome through human effort.

It is overcome through alignment with divine authority already established.

The unseen realm recognizes authority.

It responds to authority.

And where authority is exercised, occupation cannot remain permanent.

CHAPTER 19

Surveillance, Monitoring, and Spiritual Targeting

Not all observation is visible.

Some surveillance occurs beyond natural sight.

In the unseen realm, awareness of spiritual authority triggers attention. When an individual begins operating in alignment with divine purpose, resistance does not always begin with confrontation. It often begins with observation.

Monitoring precedes interference.

This monitoring is not always obvious. It manifests subtly, through patterns that appear coincidental but occur with unusual consistency.

You may notice:

• People appearing repeatedly in unexpected places
• Conversations shifting abruptly when you enter an environment
• Sudden awareness of being watched without visible cause
• Increased opposition immediately following moments of spiritual clarity

These patterns are not always random.

In spiritual warfare, surveillance serves a strategic function. It gathers information, assesses movement, and identifies potential points of influence.

However, this surveillance is limited.

Spiritual forces do not possess omniscience. They observe behavior, patterns, and responses. They study reactions. They attempt to predict actions based on previous responses.

Their effectiveness depends on predictability.

When a person operates unconsciously, they become easier to monitor. Their patterns remain consistent. Their responses remain familiar.

But when awareness increases, predictability decreases.

Unpredictability disrupts monitoring.

Alignment with divine instruction overrides external observation.

Psalm 121:7–8 provides assurance of divine protection:

"The Lord shall preserve thee from all evil: He shall preserve thy soul.
The Lord shall preserve thy going out and thy coming in from this time forth, and even for evermore."

Divine surveillance supersedes all opposition.

Where adversarial forces observe to interfere, divine authority observes to protect.

Nothing escapes divine awareness.

Surveillance by adversarial forces does not indicate vulnerability. It indicates recognition.

Recognition of assignment.

Recognition of authority.

Recognition of disruption.

Spiritual targeting does not occur randomly. It occurs where influence threatens established control.

However, targeting does not determine outcome.

Authority determines outcome.

When divine authority governs movement, surveillance becomes irrelevant.

Protection is not dependent on concealment.

Protection is dependent on alignment.

Even in monitored environments, authority remains intact.

Even in observed conditions, purpose remains unchanged.

Observation cannot override assignment.

Monitoring cannot cancel authority.

Spiritual surveillance is temporary.

Divine authority is permanent.

CHAPTER 20

Disruption of Assignment and Restoration of Authority

The objective of spiritual warfare is not always destruction.

Often, the objective is disruption.

Disruption targets movement.

It targets timing.

It targets clarity.

When direct opposition fails, disruption begins subtly. It introduces confusion, delay, distraction, and fatigue. Its purpose is not always to remove you from your assignment, but to slow your progress and weaken your momentum.

Disruption operates through interference with alignment.

You may experience:

• Unexpected delays in critical moments
• Sudden fatigue without physical explanation
• Loss of focus during periods of progress
• Interruptions that shift your attention away from purpose

These disruptions are not always visible in origin, but their intent is consistent.

They attempt to separate you from your assignment.

Assignment is the greatest threat to opposition.

When a person walks in alignment with divine authority, their movement produces impact beyond what is visible. Their presence alters environments. Their obedience initiates change.

Disruption attempts to interrupt that process.

However, disruption cannot cancel assignment.

It can only attempt to delay it.

Isaiah 54:17 provides divine confirmation:

"No weapon that is formed against thee shall prosper; and every tongue that shall rise against thee in judgment thou shalt condemn. This is the heritage of the servants of the Lord, and their righteousness is of me, saith the Lord."

Weapons may form.

Interference may occur.

But formation does not equal success.

Authority remains intact regardless of interference.

Restoration begins with realignment.

When alignment is restored, momentum returns.

Clarity returns.

Strength returns.

Assignment resumes.

Divine authority does not expire due to interruption.

It remains active.

It remains present.

It remains enforceable.

Even when progress appears delayed, assignment continues.

Nothing assigned by divine authority can be permanently disrupted by opposition.

Delay is temporary.

Authority is permanent.

Disruption is an attempt to weaken confidence.

Restoration strengthens it.

When restoration occurs, movement resumes with greater clarity and greater authority than before.

Assignment does not end because of disruption.

Assignment advances beyond it.

CHAPTER 21

Just as women face gender-specific spiritual attacks, men are targeted with warfare designed to exploit vulnerabilities unique to their calling, identity, and design.

These attacks are strategic, relentless, and often invisible—even to the men experiencing them.

Understanding how the enemy targets men is essential for recognizing and resisting these attacks.

Primary Attacks Against Men

1. Attacking Leadership and Authority

Men are wired to lead—in families, communities, churches, and workplaces. The enemy knows this and attacks:

- Confidence in decision-making
- Clarity of vision and direction
- Willingness to take responsibility
- Boldness to stand firm under pressure

When a man's leadership is undermined, everything under his covering suffers.

2. Sexual Temptation and Compromise

This is one of the most aggressive and consistent attacks against men:

- Pornography and lust
- Inappropriate relationships and emotional affairs
- Sexual sin that creates soul ties and spiritual bondage
- Shame cycles that keep men silent and isolated

Sexual sin doesn't just affect the man—it affects his family, his calling, and his spiritual authority.

3. Pride and Self-Reliance

The enemy tempts men to:

- Trust their own strength instead of God's
- Refuse to ask for help or admit weakness
- Build identity on accomplishments instead of Christ
- Compete instead of collaborate

Pride makes men unteachable, isolated, and vulnerable to spiritual collapse.

4. Passivity and Abdication

On the opposite end, the enemy also attacks men with passivity:

- Refusing to lead when leadership is needed
- Avoiding conflict or hard conversations
- Letting others carry burdens meant for them
- Disengaging from spiritual responsibility

Passive men leave their families, churches, and communities spiritually unprotected.

5. Anger and Violence

Uncontrolled anger is a weapon the enemy uses to:

- Destroy relationships
- Create fear and instability
- Damage a man's testimony and influence
- Give legal ground for demonic oppression

Anger that isn't surrendered to God becomes a tool of destruction.

How Men Can Fight Back

1. Guard Your Eyes and Your Mind

What you look at, you eventually pursue. Protect your visual and mental space from compromise.

2. Walk in Accountability

You need other men who can ask hard questions, speak truth, and hold you to your commitments.

3. Reject Passivity

Step into the leadership God has called you to—even when it's uncomfortable, even when you feel unqualified.

4. Surrender Pride

Admit when you're wrong. Ask for help. Let God be your strength.

5. Lead With Love, Not Fear

True strength isn't domination—it's sacrificial love. Lead like Christ led.

The enemy wants men weak, silent, and compromised. Refuse to cooperate.

CHAPTER 22

Coordinated Opposition

There are times when opposition doesn't come from one source—it comes from multiple directions simultaneously.

This isn't coincidence. It's coordination.

When attacks synchronize, you're dealing with organized spiritual resistance, not random conflict.

What Coordinated Opposition Looks Like

Coordinated opposition manifests as:

- Multiple people opposing you at the same time
- Problems erupting in different life areas simultaneously
- Obstacles appearing in unrelated situations with similar timing
- Resources, relationships, or opportunities being blocked from multiple angles

When you see patterns of synchronized resistance, you're not dealing with individual people—you're dealing with spiritual assignment.

The enemy coordinates attacks when:

1. You're on the Verge of Breakthrough

Increased opposition often signals imminent breakthrough. The enemy intensifies attacks to stop what's about to happen.

2. You're Operating in Your Calling

The closer you get to your assignment, the fiercer the resistance. Coordinated attacks confirm you're a threat to darkness.

3. You're Exposing Hidden Agendas

When you start seeing clearly and speaking truth, systems built on deception will coordinate to silence you.

1. Recognize It for What It Is

Don't personalize coordinated attacks. The people involved may not even realize they're being used.

2. Pray Strategically, Not Reactively

Strategic prayer targets the spiritual structure behind the coordination, not just individual situations.

3. Don't Retaliate

Your response should be spiritual, not carnal. God will defend you—you don't have to fight back in the flesh.

4. Stay Focused on Your Assignment

The goal of coordinated opposition is distraction. Refuse to be pulled off course.

5. Outlast the Resistance

Coordinated attacks are intense but not infinite. If you don't quit, the resistance will eventually break.

> **Coordinated attacks confirm your assignment. The fiercer the resistance, the greater the calling.**

Not all warfare begins with you. Some battles are inherited.

What Are Generational Patterns?

Generational patterns are spiritual, emotional, and behavioral cycles that repeat across family lines.

These include: recurring addictions, repeated trauma patterns, consistent financial struggle, recurring relationship dysfunction, spiritual blindness passed down.

These aren't genetic—they're spiritual. And they can be broken.

How Generational Patterns Form

Sin creates legal ground. Trauma creates open doors. Agreements become covenants. Silence perpetuates cycles.

When previous generations don't break free, the pattern continues—until someone decides to end it.

How to Break Generational Cycles

1. Identify the Pattern: What keeps repeating in your family line?

2. Renounce the Agreement: Reject any covenant your ancestors made with darkness.

3. Repent on Behalf of Your Lineage: Stand in the gap for those who came before you.

4. Declare Freedom: Speak freedom over yourself and future generations.

5. Live Differently: Your obedience breaks the cycle.

CHAPTER 24

Spiritual Isolation Tactics

The enemy isolates to defeat. Community strengthens.

Why Isolation Is Dangerous

Isolated believers are vulnerable believers. Without community, you have: no accountability, no correction, no encouragement, no protection, no perspective.

The enemy knows this. That's why isolation is one of his primary tactics.

How the Enemy Isolates You

Through offense and unforgiveness, creating distrust of others, making you feel misunderstood, convincing you that you're the only one who 'gets it', using pride to make you think you don't need anyone.

How to Resist Isolation

1. Stay Connected: Prioritize relationships even when it's uncomfortable.

2. Seek Community Intentionally: Don't wait for community to find you.

3. Be Vulnerable: Let people see your struggles.

4. Forgive Quickly: Don't let offense drive you into isolation.

5. Recognize the Tactic: When you feel the pull to withdraw, fight it.

CHAPTER 25

Beyond basic prayer—building impenetrable spiritual defenses.

Why Basic Prayer Isn't Always Enough

Some warfare requires advanced strategy. You need: discernment of timing, strategic fasting, spiritual covering, targeted intercession, prophetic insight.

Advanced Protection Strategies

1. Pray Preemptively, Not Just Reactively: Pray before attacks come, not just after.

2. Create Spiritual Boundaries: Limit access to your space, time, and energy.

3. Fast Strategically: Some strongholds only break through fasting and prayer.

4. Operate in Authority: Don't just ask God to do something—decree what He's already decreed.

5. Guard Your Gates: What you allow through your eyes, ears, and mouth affects your spiritual state.

CHAPTER 26

When God Is Silent

Silence doesn't mean absence. It often means preparation.

Why God Goes Silent

God's silence is not punishment—it's often preparation.

He goes silent when: testing your faith, developing spiritual maturity, breaking dependence on feelings, strengthening your trust, preparing you for what's next.

What to Do in the Silence

1. Don't Panic: Silence is not abandonment.

2. Stay Obedient: Keep doing what you know to do.

3. Review What God Already Said: Go back to previous instruction.

4. Wait Expectantly: Something is coming—God is working even when you can't see it.

The silence will break. Stay faithful.

CHAPTER 27

Not all calm is from God. Some peace is a setup.

What Is False Peace?

False peace is calm that comes from compromise, not surrender.

It feels like relief, but it's actually spiritual numbness.

False peace says: 'Stop resisting', 'This is fine', 'You're overreacting'.

How to Recognize False Peace

True peace: Comes with clarity, aligns with God's Word, brings freedom, strengthens conviction.

False peace: Requires compromise, contradicts Scripture, brings numbness, weakens discernment.

If peace requires you to ignore what God showed you—it's false.

The Power of Fasting

Fasting breaks what prayer alone can't touch.

Why Fasting Matters

Fasting is not about proving devotion—it's about breaking strongholds.

Jesus said some things only come out through prayer and fasting.

Fasting: sharpens discernment, weakens the flesh, strengthens the spirit, breaks demonic resistance, accelerates breakthrough.

How to Fast Strategically

1. Fast With Purpose: Know what you're fasting for.

2. Choose the Right Fast: Food, media, technology—whatever creates dependence.

3. Replace What You Remove: Fill fasting time with prayer, worship, and Scripture.

4. Expect Resistance: The enemy will try to break your fast.

5. Break the Fast Wisely: Return to normal slowly and intentionally.

CHAPTER 29

Spiritual Endurance

Warfare isn't a sprint. It's sustained resistance.

Why Endurance Matters

Many believers start strong but don't finish.

The enemy knows this. He doesn't always need to defeat you—he just needs to outlast you.

Spiritual endurance is the ability to keep going when breakthrough hasn't come yet.

How to Build Endurance

1. Pace Yourself: Don't burn out in the first round.

2. Celebrate Small Wins: Progress is still progress.

3. Rest Strategically: Rest is not retreat—it's refueling.

4. Remember Past Victories: God has brought you through before.

5. Keep Your Eyes on the Finish Line: Don't quit before the breakthrough.

CHAPTER 30

Building spiritual stability that attacks can't penetrate.

What Does Unshakeable Mean?

Unshakeable doesn't mean attacks stop—it means they don't move you.

It means: your foundation is firm, your identity is secure, your discernment is sharp, your authority is activated, your peace is unshakeable.

How to Become Unshakeable

1. Build on the Rock: Obedience to God's Word creates unshakeable foundation.

2. Know Who You Are: Identity rooted in Christ can't be stolen.

3. Practice Discernment Daily: The more you exercise it, the stronger it gets.

4. Stay Connected to God: Unshakeable people stay in His presence.

5. Outlast Every Attack: You become unshakeable by refusing to be shaken.

CHAPTER 31

Your Assignment and Opposition

The stronger your calling, the fiercer the resistance.

Why Opposition Confirms Assignment

If you're facing fierce resistance, it's because you're a threat to darkness.

The enemy doesn't waste energy attacking people who aren't a threat.

Opposition isn't proof you're off track—it's often proof you're on it.

How to Navigate Opposition

1. Don't Let Opposition Define You: Your assignment defines you, not your resistance.

2. Expect Warfare: Stop being surprised by attacks.

3. Stay Focused: Opposition's goal is distraction—refuse to be pulled off course.

4. Trust God's Timing: Your assignment will be fulfilled—keep walking.

The fiercer the opposition, the greater the calling.

CHAPTER 32

Final Strategies

Advanced tactics for those who refuse to quit.

Final Strategic Principles

1. Operate in Your Authority: Stop asking for what you already have—use it.

2. Don't Fight Alone: Build a prayer team who covers you.

3. Document Patterns: Write down what you're seeing—patterns reveal strategy.

4. Trust Your Discernment: Stop second-guessing what God has shown you.

5. Never Stop Learning: Spiritual warfare evolves—so should your strategy.

A Final Word on Strategy

You don't need more information—you need more implementation.

Everything you need to win has already been given to you.

Now it's time to walk it out.

CHAPTER 33

Walking in Total Freedom

Living fully awakened and completely free.

What Total Freedom Looks Like

Total freedom isn't the absence of warfare—it's the presence of unshakeable peace in the midst of it.

Free people: see clearly without fear, discern without paranoia, walk in authority without arrogance, love without naivety, rest in God's sovereignty.

How to Maintain Freedom

1. Guard What You've Gained: Freedom requires maintenance.

2. Stay in Community: Isolation invites bondage back in.

3. Keep Learning: Complacency creates vulnerability.

4. Walk in Humility: Pride opens doors you've already closed.

5. Live From Victory, Not For Victory: You're already free—live like it.

Final Encouragement

You were not meant to live in fear, confusion, or oppression.

You were created to walk in freedom, clarity, and authority.

You are awake. You are equipped. You are free.

Now go live like it.

www.ingramcontent.com/pod-product-compliance
Lightning Source LLC
Chambersburg PA
CBHW052018150726
47999CB00004B/1709